D0049529

# A Bouquet of Flowers

To _____

From _____

# A Bouquet of Flowers

BY
BARBARA MILO OHRBACH

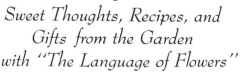

*Sweet Thoughts, Recipes, and
Gifts from the Garden
with "The Language of Flowers"*

CLARKSON N. POTTER, INC./PUBLISHERS
NEW YORK

Design by Justine Strasberg          Endpapers by Rita Singer

Publisher's Note: This book contains several potpourri recipes, using dried flowers, herbs, and other natural ingredients. Some of these components may cause allergic reactions in some individuals, so reasonable care in preparation is advised.

Every effort has been made to locate the copyright holders of materials used in this book. Should there be any omissions or errors, we apologize and shall be pleased to make the appropriate acknowledgments in future editions.

Grateful acknowledgment is made to the following for permission to reprint previously published material: Harper & Row, Publishers, Inc.: an excerpt from COLLECTED POEMS OF EDNA SAINT VINCENT MILLAY. Copyright 1956 by Norma Millay Ellis. Reprinted by permission of Harper & Row, Publishers, Inc. Houghton Mifflin Company: an excerpt from THE COMPLETE POETICAL WORKS OF AMY LOWELL. Copyright © 1955 by Houghton Mifflin Company. Copyright © 1983 renewed by Houghton Mifflin Company, Brinton P. Roberts, Esquire, and G. D'Andelot Belin, Esquire. Reprinted by permission of Houghton Mifflin Company. Jerry Vogel Music Company, Inc.: an excerpt from Joyce Kilmer's TREES used by permission of the Copyright owner. Liveright Publishing Corporation: lines from "this is the garden: colours come and go," are reprinted from TULIPS & CHIMNEYS by E. E. Cummings, Edited by George James Firmage, by permission of Liveright Publishing Company. Copyright 1923, 1925 and renewed 1951, 1953 by E. E. Cummings. Copyright © 1973, 1976 by the Trustees for the E. E. Cummings Trust. Copyright © 1973, 1976 by George James Firmage.

Published by Clarkson N. Potter, Inc., distributed by Crown Publishers, Inc., 201 East 50th Street, New York, New York 10022

CLARKSON N. POTTER, POTTER, and colophon are trademarks of Clarkson N. Potter, Inc.

Manufactured in Japan

Library of Congress Catalog Card Number: 90-6840

ISBN 0-517-57428-4

10  9  8  7  6  5  4  3  2  1

First Edition

# Table of Contents

To *Aunt Jeanette and Lee*
*and the other green thumbs in my family*

Special thanks and a bouquet of flowers that includes Bell Flowers (Gratitude), Morning Glorys (Affection), Bluebells (Constancy), and Magnolias (Love of Nature), for each person who helped on this little book:

Everyone at Clarkson N. Potter, especially Gretchen Salisbury, Dania Martinez Davey, Valerie Borchardt, María Bottino, and Brenda Goldberg. ❦ Justine Strasburg, for her sweet point of view. ❦ Deborah Geltman, who follows up and follows up. ❦ Everyone at Cherchez, especially Lisa Fresne and Gloria Schaaf. ❦ All the people whose delightful thoughts on the green world around us appear here.

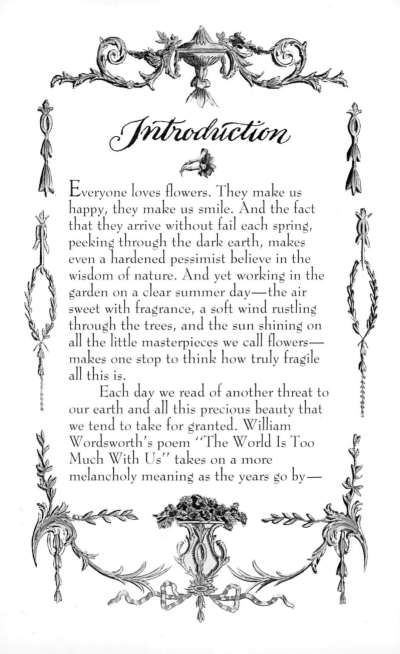

# Introduction

Everyone loves flowers. They make us happy, they make us smile. And the fact that they arrive without fail each spring, peeking through the dark earth, makes even a hardened pessimist believe in the wisdom of nature. And yet working in the garden on a clear summer day—the air sweet with fragrance, a soft wind rustling through the trees, and the sun shining on all the little masterpieces we call flowers— makes one stop to think how truly fragile all this is.

Each day we read of another threat to our earth and all this precious beauty that we tend to take for granted. William Wordsworth's poem "The World Is Too Much With Us" takes on a more melancholy meaning as the years go by—

*The world is too much with us; late and soon,*
*Getting and spending, we lay waste our powers:*
*Little we see in Nature that is ours.*

I thought of this often when I was gathering quotes for *A Bouquet of Flowers.* A collection of wise, loving, sometimes wry, and often profound thoughts, it is about all these things in nature that sustain our spirits. The authors, from Abraham Lincoln to Colette, express a special affection for flowers, gardens— really, everything growing around us.

Included also is "The Language of Flowers." A way of communicating through flowers with someone you cared about, it was popular in a quieter time and might be worth reviving today.

Many of us like the idea of living in harmony with nature and think it essential for a happy and satisfied life. What each of us *does* to protect this fragile and beautiful world matters. I dearly hope that hundreds of years from now flowers and the world around us will be written about as touchingly and optimistically as they have been in the past.

Barbara Milo Ohrbach
New York City

To see the world in a grain of sand,
And a heaven in a wild flower;
Hold infinity in the palm of your hand,
And eternity in an hour.

WILLIAM BLAKE

The year's at the spring
And day's at the morn;
Morning's at seven;
The hill-side's dew-pearled;
The lark's on the wing;

The snail's on the thorn:
God's in his heaven—
All's right with the world!

ROBERT BROWNING

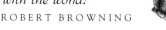

1

Arranging a bowl of flowers in the morning
can give a sense of quiet in a crowded day—
like writing a poem, or saying a prayer.

ANNE MORROW LINDBERGH

# A Garden Bouquet

*Picking and working with flowers can be a pleasurable and satisfying experience. Here are some tips on the gentle care of cut flowers.*

🌢 Cut flowers in early morning, if possible, when the scent is strongest.

🌢 When cutting flowers, especially in very hot weather, soak them for an hour or two in deep, cool water, then arrange them in a vase.

🌢 Constance Spry suggests cutting flowers the day before they are required.

🌢 Always use a sharp knife or florist's shears when cutting stems.

🌢 Cut stems on an angle to increase the area through which the plant takes in water.

🌢 Hard-wooded flowers (like lilacs) should have their stems crushed with a hammer before being put in water.

🌢 Remove excess leaves from all flowers. Flowers can suffer from overhandling and temperature changes, so replace the water only when necessary to prevent a stagnant odor.

To-day man sows the cause, and God
to-morrow ripens the effect.

VICTOR HUGO

Who loves a Garden loves a Greenhouse too.

WILLIAM COWPER

If I had but two loaves of bread, I would sell one
and buy hyacinths, for they would feed my soul.

THE KORAN

Once I had plants and no money—now what is
money good for, without plants?

LINNAEUS

I count my blessings with the flowers, never with
the leaves that fall.

LADY BIRD JOHNSON

Consider the lilies of the field, how they
grow; they toil not, neither do they spin.

MATTHEW

March winds and April showers
bring forth May flowers.

PROVERBIAL SAYING

Let others tell of rain and showers;
I only count the shining hours.

SUNDIAL INSCRIPTION

Supreme he stands among the flowers
And only marks Life's sunny hours.
For him dull days do not exist—
The brazen-faced old optimist.

SUNDIAL INSCRIPTION

5

Our garden is now a wilderness of sweets.
The violets, sweet briar, and primroses perfume
the air, and the thrushes are full of melody and
make our concert complete. It is the pleasantest
music I have heard this year, and refreshes my
spirits without the alloy of a tumultuous crowd,
which attends all the other concerts.

MRS. DELANY

## Candied Violets and Roses

Crystallized or candied flowers lend an evocative touch to what would normally be considered a simple dessert. Use them to decorate scoops of sherbet, or to create a design on an iced cake.

FRESH VIOLET BLOSSOMS
PINK ROSE PETALS
EGG WHITES

SUGAR, FINELY
GRANULATED

🌺 Pick the flowers fresh in the early morning. Gently wash and pat dry.

🌺 Pour the sugar into one bowl. Beat the egg whites into another bowl.

🌺 Carefully dip the flowers and petals into the egg whites. Then roll them in sugar, being sure to cover all sides adequately.

🌺 Set the petals and flowers on a cookie sheet to dry in a warm place.

🌺 Store in a rectangular plastic container with waxed paper between layers. They will last for several days.

🌺 Leaves of herbs such as lemon verbena and mint may be candied in the same way.

He who would have beautiful Roses in his garden must have beautiful Roses in his heart.

DEAN HOLE

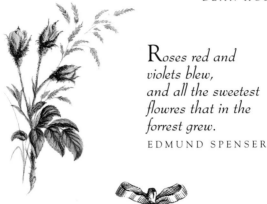

Roses red and violets blew, and all the sweetest flowres that in the forrest grew.

EDMUND SPENSER

One is nearer God's heart in a garden than anywhere else on earth.

DOROTHY FRANCES GURNEY

 And I will make thee beds of roses, and a thousand fragrant posies.

CHRISTOPHER MARLOWE

That which we call a rose By any other name would smell as sweet.

WILLIAM SHAKESPEARE

Each Morn a thousand Roses brings,
	you say;
Yes, but where leaves the Rose of
	Yesterday?

OMAR KHAYYÁM

God has given us our memories that
we might have roses in December.

J.M. BARRIE

Every blade of grass, each leaf, each separate
floret and petal, is an inscription speaking of
hope.

RICHARD JEFFERIES

'Tis the last rose of summer
	Left blooming alone;
All her lovely companions
	Are faded and gone.

THOMAS MOORE

We must cultivate our garden.

VOLTAIRE

*Flowers that their gay wardrobe wear.*

JOHN MILTON

## Sweet Dreams Sachets

For hundreds of years, certain herbs and flowers were thought to have sleep-inducing qualities. Whether they really work is debatable, but they certainly smell heavenly, putting us in a much more gentle mood. This charming recipe is from the seventeenth century.

1 CUP DRIED ROSE PETALS

½ CUP DRIED MINT

2 TABLESPOONS WHOLE CLOVES

1 TABLESPOON GROUND CLOVES

5 DROPS ROSE OIL

6 SMALL MUSLIN OR COTTON BAGS

❧ Combine the herbs and rose oil in a bowl.

❧ Spoon the mixture into the bags, tying at the top with a pretty ribbon.

❧ Tuck into a corner of your pillowcase or tie onto the bedpost where the scent will linger.

MAKES 6 SMALL SACHETS

Flowers are restful to look at. They have neither emotions nor conflicts.

SIGMUND FREUD

Sweet flowers are slow and weeds make haste.

WILLIAM SHAKESPEARE

Consult the genius of the place.

ALEXANDER POPE

How often I regret that plants cannot talk.

VITA SACKVILLE-WEST

Green fingers are the extensions of a verdant heart.

RUSSELL PAGE

I love not man the less, but nature more.

GEORGE GORDON, LORD BYRON

Nothing is more the child of art than a garden.

SIR WALTER SCOTT

The honisuckle that groweth wilde in every hedge, although it be very sweete, yet doe I not bring it into my garden, but let it reste in his owne place, to serve their senses that travell by it, or have no garden.

JOHN PARKINSON

Lilacs in dooryards
Holding quiet conversations with an early moon.

AMY LOWELL

Just now the lilac is in bloom,
All before my little room;
And in my flower-beds, I think,
Smile the carnation and the pink

RUPERT BROOKE

In his garden every man may be his own artist without apology or explanation. Here is one spot where each may experience the "romance of possibility."

LOUISE BEEBE WILDER

I do not envy the owners of very large gardens.
The garden should fit its master or his tastes,
just as his clothes do; it should be neither too
large nor too small, but just comfortable.

GERTRUDE JEKYLL

# Fresh Herb Ice Cubes

$T$*his is an appealing idea
that can make the simplest glass of iced tea or
lemonade into a sophisticated and tangy offering
for unexpected guests.*

1 INCH SPRIGS OR
   LEAVES OF ANY OF THE
   FOLLOWING HERBS:
   LEMON VERBENA
   LEMON BALM
   PEPPERMINT
   LEMON MINT
   ORANGE MINT

   APPLE MINT
   SPEARMINT OR
   PINEAPPLE MINT
1 LEMON
   ICE CUBE TRAYS WITH
   INTERESTING SHAPES

❧ Pick the herbs in early morning when they
are most fragrant.

❧ Break off 1 inch sprigs or individual leaves.

❧ Wash them thoroughly, and drain carefully
so that leaves do not get crushed or broken.

❧ Fill a pitcher with water and squeeze the
lemon into it; stir.

❧ Fill the ice cube tray with the water and
submerge one sprig or leaf per cube, so that it is
completely covered. Freeze.

More than half a century has passed, and yet each spring, when I wander into the primrose wood and see the pale yellow blooms, and smell their sweetest of scents, . . . for a moment I am seven years old again and wandering in the fragrant wood.

GERTRUDE JEKYLL

Die when I may, I want it said of me by those who know me best, that I always plucked a thistle and planted a flower where I thought a flower would grow.

ABRAHAM LINCOLN

We Englishmen talk of planting a garden; the modern Italians and ancient Romans talk of building one—as though the architect's garden were utterly unknown in England.

WALTER SAVAGE LANDOR

Nature, to be commanded, must be obeyed.

FRANCIS BACON

Cowslips, like topazes that shine,
Close by the silver serpentine,
Rude rustics which assert the bow'rs
Amidst the educated flow'rs.

CHRISTOPHER SMART

What a man needs
in gardening is a
cast-iron back, with a
hinge in it.

CHARLES DUDLEY WARNER

Flowers are the sweetest things God ever
made and forgot to put a soul into.

HENRY WARD BEECHER

Let us give therefore to Gardens their due honor;
and let us not, (I say) deprive things of their
credit and authoritie, because they are common
and nothing costly.

PLINY

17

*In emerald tufts, flowers purple, blue,*
*and white;*
*Like sapphire, pearl, and rich embroidery.*

WILLIAM SHAKESPEARE

18

## Scented Note Papers

$A$n old-fashioned idea that has become popular again is the romantic notion of scenting your stationery. It makes each note you send a little bit more personal.

8 OUNCES OF UNSCENTED TALCUM POWDER

15 DROPS OF YOUR FAVORITE PERFUME OR ESSENTIAL OIL

6 SMALL, CLOSELY WOVEN, PRETTY COTTON OR SILK BAGS

❧ Mix the talcum powder and perfume in a bowl. Cover with foil and let sit for one day.

❧ Spoon the mixture into the bags and tie with pretty ribbon.

❧ Place the bags in between the layers of notepaper and envelopes in a box.

❧ Put the box in a plastic bag so that the scent permeates the paper. This will take several days.

MAKES ABOUT 6 SACHETS

Birds of a feather will gather together.

SIR RICHARD BURTON

I once had a sparrow alight upon my shoulder, while hoeing in a village garden, and I felt I was more distinguished by that circumstance than I should have been by any epaulet I could have worn.

HENRY DAVID THOREAU

Hope is the thing with feathers
That perches in the soul,
And sings the tune without the words,
And never stops at all.

EMILY DICKINSON

The flowers appear on the earth;
the time of the singing of birds is come.

SONG OF SOLOMON

I was always a lover of soft-winged things.

VICTOR HUGO

The mute bird sitting on the stone,
The dank moss dripping from the wall,
The garden-walk with weeds o'ergrown,
I love them—how I love them all!

EMILY BRONTË

A bird in the hand is worth two in the bush.

MIGUEL DE CERVANTES SAAVEDRA

Hear how the birds, on ev'ry
blooming spray,
With joyous musick wake the
dawning day!

ALEXANDER POPE

There was never mystery
But 'tis figured in the flowers;
Was never secret history
But birds tell it in the bowers.

RALPH WALDO EMERSON

What do we plant when we plant the tree?
A thousand things that we daily see;
We plant the spire that out-towers the crag,
We plant the staff for our country's flag,
We plant the shade, from the hot sun free;
We plant all these when we plant the tree.

HENRY ABBEY

Even if I knew certainly the world would end
tomorrow, I would plant an apple tree today.

MARTIN LUTHER

He who plants a tree,—
He plants love.

LUCY LARCOM

He that plants a tree loves others besides himself.

If a tree dies, plant another in its place.

LINNAEUS

Loveliest of trees, the cherry now
Is hung with bloom along the bough,
And stands about the woodland ride
Wearing white for Eastertide.

A.E. HOUSMAN

In small proportions we just beauties see,
And in short measures life may perfect be.

BEN JONSON

I think that I shall never see
A poem lovely as a tree.

JOYCE KILMER

We cannot fathom the mystery of a single flower, nor is it intended that we should; but that the pursuit of science should constantly be betrayed by the love of beauty, and accuracy of knowledge by tenderness of emotion.

JOHN RUSKIN

# The Language of Flowers

The Language of Flowers, oriental in origin, was introduced to England by Lady Mary Wortley Montagu in the mid-eighteenth century. In her letters from Constantinople, where her husband was ambassador, she wrote that "There is no color, no flower, no weed, no fruit, herb, pebble or feather that has not a verse belonging to it. . . . You may send letters of passion, friendship, or civility without inking your fingers."

The Language of Flowers, most popular in Europe, evolved into a list of sentimental meanings and thoughts in which each flower had a particular significance. For example, a nosegay composed of globe amaranth (unfading love), bluebell (constancy), clover (be mine), and roses (love) would be an affectionate gift of flowers indeed.

So, if you like this idea as much as I do, find yourself a piece of lovely old ribbon, go out into the garden and make a special bouquet for someone you care about.

ACACIA, PINK . . . . . . . . . . . . . *Elegance*

ALMOND, FLOWERING . . . . . . . *Hope*

AMARANTH, GLOBE . . . . . . . . . *Unfading love*

AMARYLLIS . . . . . . . . . . . . . . . *Pride*

AMBROSIA . . . . . . . . . . . . . . . . *Love returned*

ANEMONE, GARDEN . . . . . . . . . *Forsaken*

ANGELICA . . . . . . . . . . . . . . . *Inspiration*

APPLE BLOSSOM . . . . . . . . . . . *Preference*

ASTER, CHINA . . . . . . . . . . . . . *Variety*

AURICULA . . . . . . . . . . . . . . . . *Importune me not*

AZALEA . . . . . . . . . . . . . . . . . *Temperance*

BACHELOR'S BUTTONS . . . . . . *Single blessedness*

BALM . . . . . . . . . . . . . . . . . . *Sympathy*

BAY . . . . . . . . . . . . . . . . . . *Glory*

BEGONIA . . . . . . . . . . . . . . . . *Dark thoughts*

BELL FLOWER . . . . . . . . . . . . . *Gratitude*

BITTERSWEET . . . . . . . . . . . . . *Truth*

BLUEBELL . . . . . . . . . . . . . . . . *Constancy*

BORAGE . . . . . . . . . . . . . . . . . *Bluntness*

BUTTERCUP . . . . . . . . . . . . . . . *Childishness*

CAMELLIA, WHITE . . . . . . . . . *Perfected loveliness*

CAMOMILE . . . . . . . . . . . . . . *Energy in adversity*

CAMPANULA . . . . . . . . . . . . . *Gratitude*

CANTERBURY BELL . . . . . . . . . *Acknowledgment*

CARNATION, RED . . . . . . . . . . *Alas my poor heart*

CHRYSANTHEMUM, RED . . . . . *I love*

CLEMATIS . . . . . . . . . . . . . . . . . *Mental beauty*
CLOVER, FOUR-LEAVED . . . . . . *Be mine*
CLOVER, WHITE . . . . . . . . . . . *Think of me*
COCKSCOMB . . . . . . . . . . . . . . *Singularity*
COLUMBINE . . . . . . . . . . . . . . . *Folly*
COLUMBINE, PURPLE . . . . . . . *Resolution*
CONVOLVULUS . . . . . . . . . . . . . *Uncertainty*
COREOPSIS . . . . . . . . . . . . *Always cheerful*
COWSLIP . . . . . . . . . . . . . . . . *Pensiveness*
CROCUS, SPRING . . . . . . . . . . *Youthful gladness*
CYCLAMEN . . . . . . . . . . . . . . *Diffidence*
DAFFODIL . . . . . . . . . . . . . . *Regard*
DAHLIA . . . . . . . . . . . . . . . . *Good taste*
DAISY . . . . . . . . . . . . . . . . . *Innocence*
DOCK . . . . . . . . . . . . . . . . . *Patience*
DOGWOOD . . . . . . . . . . . . . . *Durability*
FLAX . . . . . . . . . . . . . . . . *Fate*
FORGET-ME-NOT . . . . . . . . . . . *True love*
FOXGLOVE . . . . . . . . . . . . . . . *Insincerity*
FRENCH HONEYSUCKLE . . . . . . *Rustic beauty*
GARDEN CHERVIL . . . . . . . . . . *Sincerity*
GENTIAN . . . . . . . . . . . . . . . . *You are unjust*
GERANIUM, ROSE-SCENTED . . . *Preference*
GERANIUM, SCARLET . . . . . . . *Comforting*
GILLIFLOWER . . . . . . . . . . . . *Lasting beauty*
GLADIOLA . . . . . . . . . . . . . . *Strong character*

Lastly, love your flowers. By some subtle sense the dear things always detect their friends, and for them they will live longer and bloom more freely than they ever will for a stranger.

JULIA S. BERRALL

| | |
|---|---|
| GLOXINIA | *A proud spirit* |
| HELIOTROPE | *Devotion* |
| HIBISCUS | *Delicate beauty* |
| HOLLYHOCK | *Ambition* |
| HONEYSUCKLE | *Devoted affection* |
| HYACINTH | *Sport, game, play* |
| HYDRANGEA | *Heartlessness* |
| HYSSOP | *Cleanliness* |
| IRIS | *Message* |
| IVY | *Fidelity* |
| JACOB'S LADDER | *Come down* |
| JASMINE, WHITE | *Amiability* |
| JASMINE, YELLOW | *Grace and elegance* |
| JONQUIL | *I desire a return of affection* |
| LADY'S SLIPPER | *Capricious beauty* |
| LANTANA | *Rigour* |
| LARKSPUR | *Lightness, levity* |
| LAUREL | *Glory* |
| LAVENDER | *Distrust* |
| LILAC, PURPLE | *Love's first emotions* |
| LILAC, WHITE | *Youthful innocence* |
| LILY, WHITE | *Purity, sweetness* |
| LILY-OF-THE-VALLEY | *Return of happiness* |
| LOVE-IN-A-MIST | *Perplexity* |

LUPINE . . . . . . . . . . . . . . . . . . . . *Voraciousness*

MAGNOLIA . . . . . . . . . . . *Love of nature*

MARIGOLD . . . . . *Grief*

MARJORAM . . . . . . . . . . . . . . *Blushes*

MEADOWSWEET . . . . . . . . . . . *Uselessness*

MIGNONETTE . . . . . . . . . . . . . *Your qualities sur-
                                        pass your charms*

MIMOSA . . . . . . *Sensitiveness*

MINT . . . . . . . . . . . . . . . . . . . . *Virtue*

MOCK ORANGE . . . . . . . . . . . *Counterfeit*

MORNING GLORY . . . . . . . . . . *Affection*

MUGWORT . . . . . . . . . . . . . . . *Happiness*

MYRTLE . . . . . . . . . . . . . . . . . . *Love*

NARCISSUS . . . . . . . . . . *Egotism*

NASTURTIUM . . . . . . . . . . . . *Patriotism*

ORANGE BLOSSOMS . . . . . . . . *Bridal festivities*

PANSY . . . . . . . . . . . . . . . . . . . . *Thinking of you*

PARSLEY . . . . . . . . . . . . . . *Festivity*

PEA, SWEET . . . . . . . . . . . . *Lasting pleasures*

PEACH BLOSSOM . . . . . . . . . . . *I am your captive*

PENNYROYAL . . . . . . . . . . . *Flee away*

PEONY . . . . . . . . . . . . . . . . . . . *Bashfulness*

PEPPERMINT . . . . . . . . *Warmth of feeling*

PERIWINKLE, BLUE . . . . . . . . . *Early friendship*

PERIWINKLE, WHITE . . . . . . . . *Pleasures of
                                        memory*

| | |
|---|---|
| PETUNIA | *Never despair* |
| PHLOX | *Unanimity* |
| PINK | *Boldness* |
| POLYANTHUS | *Pride of riches* |
| POPPY, RED | *Consolation* |
| PRIMROSE | *Early youth* |
| PRIMULA | *Diffidence* |
| QUINCE | *Temptation* |
| RANUNCULUS | *You are radiant with charms* |
| ROSE | *Love* |
| ROSE, CABBAGE | *Ambassador of love* |
| ROSE, CHINA | *Beauty always new* |
| ROSE, DAMASK | *Brilliant complexion* |
| ROSE, MUNDI | *Variety* |
| ROSE, MUSK | *Capricious beauty* |
| ROSE, RED AND WHITE TOGETHER | *Unity* |
| ROSEBUD, RED | *Pure and lovely* |
| ROSEMARY | *Remembrance* |
| SAGE, GARDEN | *Esteem* |
| SALVIA, BLUE | *I think of you* |
| SALVIA, RED | *Forever thine* |
| SCILLA, BLUE | *Forgive and forget* |
| SNAPDRAGON | *No* |
| SORREL | *Affection* |

*I am painting now with the rapture of a Marseillais eating bouillabaisse, which will not surprise you when you hear that the subject is big sunflowers. I am working on them every morning, starting at daybreak—for they fade quickly. . . .*

VINCENT VAN GOGH

SPEARMINT . . . . . . . . . . . . . . . *Warmth of sentiment*

STEPHANOTIS . . . . . . . . . . . . . *You can boast*
*too much*

STOCK . . . . . . . . . . . . . . . . . *Lasting beauty*

SUNFLOWER, DWARF . . . . . . . *Adoration*

SWEET BASIL . . . . . . . . . . . . . . *Good wishes*

SWEET BRIAR . . . . . . . . . . . . . *Simplicity*

SWEET PEA . . . . . . . . . . . . . . *Delicate pleasures*

SWEET WILLIAM . . . . . . . . . . *Gallantry*

SYRINGA . . . . . . . . . . . . . . *Memory*

THYME . . . . . . . . . . . . . . . . *Activity*

TRILLIUM PICTUM . . . . . . . . . *Modest beauty*

TRUMPET FLOWER . . . . . . . . . *Fame*

TUBEROSE . . . . . . . . . . . . . . . *Dangerous pleasures*

TULIP, RED . . . . . . . . . . . . . . . *Declaration of love*

TULIP, VARIEGATED . . . . . . . . *Beautiful eyes*

TULIP, YELLOW . . . . . . . . . . *Hopeless love*

VERBENA, WHITE . . . . . . . . . *Pure and guileless*

VERONICA . . . . . . . . . . . . . . . *Fidelity*

VIOLET, BLUE . . . . . . . . . . . . . *Faithfulness*

WALLFLOWER . . . . . . . . . . . . . *Fidelity in adversity*

WISTERIA . . . . . . . . . . . . . . . *I cling to thee,*
*welcome*

WOODBINE . . . . . . . . . . . . . . *Fraternal love*

ZINNIA . . . . . . . . . . . . . . . . . *Thoughts of an*
*absent friend*

Apples and quinces,
    Lemons and oranges,
Plump unpecked cherries,
    Melons and raspberries,
Bloom-down-cheeked peaches,
    Swart-headed mulberries,
Wild free-born cranberries,
    Crab-apples, dewberries,
Pine-apples, blackberries,
    Apricots, strawberries;
All ripe together
    In summer weather.

CHRISTINA ROSSETTI

I will be the gladdest thing under the sun!
I will touch a hundred flowers and not pick one.

EDNA SAINT VINCENT MILLAY

I do not want change. I want the same old and loved things, the same trees and soft ash-green; the turtle-doves, the blackbirds, the coloured yellow-hammer sing, sing, singing so long as there is light to cast a shadow on the dial, for such is the measure of his song, and I want them in the same place.

RICHARD JEFFERIES

And 'tis my faith that every flower
Enjoys the air it breathes.

WILLIAM WORDSWORTH

I've often wished that I had clear,
For life, six hundred pounds a year;
A handsome house to lodge a friend,
A river at my garden's end,
A terrace walk, and half a rood
Of land set out to plant a wood.

ALEXANDER POPE

I am just come out of the garden on the most oriental of all evenings, and from breathing odours beyond those of Araby.

HORACE WALPOLE

We should be blessed if we lived in the present always, and took advantage of every accident that befell us, like the grass which confesses the influence of the slightest dew that falls on it. . . . We loiter in winter while it is already spring.

HENRY DAVID THOREAU

I value my garden more for being full of blackbirds than cherries, and very frankly give them fruits for their songs.

JOSEPH ADDISON

A garden is not for giving or taking. A garden is for all.

F.H. BURNETT

Some people like to make a little garden out of life and walk down a path.

JEAN ANOUILH

Patience is a flower that grows not in everyone's garden.

OLD PROVERB

When the well's dry, we know the worth of water.

BENJAMIN FRANKLIN

Whatever a man's age, he can reduce it several years by putting a bright-colored flower in his buttonhole.

MARK TWAIN

"I left London by the Comet coach and arrived at half-past 4 o'clock in the morning. As no person was to be seen at that early hour I got over the greenhouse gates by the old covered way, explored the pleasure grounds and looked round the outside of the house . . . afterwards went to breakfast with poor dear Mrs. Gregory and her niece; the latter fell in love with me and I with her, and thus completed my first morning's work at Chatsworth before 9 o'clock."

JOSEPH PAXTON

# Summer Flower Salads

We all use fresh herbs in our salads as a matter of course, but using flowers adds an element of surprise and color, too. As early as the fifteenth century, flowers were planted in kitchen gardens. The following flowers can be used to deliciously garnish summer salads as well as other foods.

NASTURTIUMS ❦ Use the whole yellowy orange blossoms and green leaves for a peppery flavor in soups.

ROSES ❦ Use the pink and red petals for a subtle, sweet flavor in desserts.

BORAGE ❦ Use the whole blue flower, which tastes a little like cucumber, in fruit cups or ices.

MARIGOLDS ❦ Use the bright, orange petals for a saffron flavor in vegetables and poultry.

SQUASH FLOWERS ❦ The large, orange flowers have a subtle bouquet and can be stuffed or fried.

The bee is little among such things as fly; but her fruit is the chief of sweet things.

ECCLESIASTICUS

The pedigree of honey
Does not concern the bee;
A clover, any time, to him
Is aristocracy.

EMILY DICKINSON

"Just living is not enough,"
said the butterfly. "One must have sunshine,
freedom, and a little flower."

HANS CHRISTIAN ANDERSEN

We once had a lily here that bore 108 flowers on one stalk: It was photographed naturally for all the gardening papers. The bees came from miles and miles, and there were the most disgraceful Bacchanalian scenes: bees hardly able to find their way home.

EDITH SITWELL

It was a lovely day of blue skies and gentle breezes. Bees buzzed, birds tootled, and squirrels bustled to and fro, getting their sun-tan in the bright sunshine. In a word all Nature smiled.

P. G. WODEHOUSE

All the names I know from nurse:
Gardener's garters, Shepherd's purse,
Bachelor's buttons, Lady's smock,
And the Lady Hollyhock.

ROBERT LOUIS STEVENSON

As for rosemarie I lette it runne all over my garden walls, not onlie because my bees love it, but because it is the herb sacred to remembrance and to friendship, whence a sprig of it hath a dumb language.

SIR THOMAS MORE

A rose is a rose is a rose is a rose.

GERTRUDE STEIN

## Garden Rose Finger Bowls

*D*etails *are so important.*
*Though none of us entertains as much as we*
*would like, when we do, all the little touches*
*should be there.*

1 CUP STRONGLY
SCENTED ROSE PETALS

4 CUPS DISTILLED
WATER

6 DROPS ROSE OIL

6 FRESHLY PICKED
WHOLE ROSE HEADS
FROM THE GARDEN

❧ Pick the rose petals in early morning when the scent is strongest.

❧ Boil the water, add the rose petals and oil, and set aside to cool.

❧ When cool, strain and discard the petals.

❧ Fill each finger bowl half full with the fragrantly scented water.

❧ Just before guests arrive, add 1 whole rose head to each finger bowl. Place them at each setting when you serve dessert.

❧ As a variation, use violets or sweet peas with oil of the same scent.

MAKES 6 BOWLS

The first sparrow of spring! The year beginning
with
younger hope than ever!

HENRY DAVID THOREAU

Spring hangs her infant
blossoms on the trees,
Rock'd in the cradle of the
western breeze.

WILLIAM COWPER

O gift of God! a perfect day,
Whereon shall no man work but play,
Whereon it is enough for me
Not to be doing but to be.

HENRY WADSWORTH LONGFELLOW

Never does nature
say one thing and
wisdom another.

JUVENAL

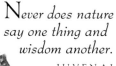

All for the love of flowers.

LINNAEUS

*this is the garden: colours come and go,*
*frail azures fluttering from night's outer wing*
*strong silent greens serenely lingering,*
*absolute lights like baths of golden snow.*

E.E. CUMMINGS

The world's favorite season
is in the spring.
All things are possible in May.

EDWIN WAY TEALE

There's something good
in all weathers. If it don't happen
to be good for my work to-day, it's
good for some other man's.

CHARLES DICKENS

"My little plot," said Miss Mapp.
"My flower beds: sweet roses,
tortoiseshell butterflies. Rather
a nice clematis. My little
Eden, I call it, so small but
so well beloved."

E.F. BENSON

We push open the grilled-iron gate, gilded and black, and the world changes. We are in a springtime so fairylike that one trembles lest it sink and dissolve in a mist. The fountain, Diana's bath; deep avenues of stone where roars an imperious green water, transparent, dark, blue and brilliant. . . .

COLETTE

## Soothing Bath Bags

Pampering yourself with an herbal bath is always relaxing and rejuvenating. Adding oatmeal to the recipe makes the water feel soft and silky, and the herbs smell nice, too.

1 CUP OATMEAL
½ CUP OF ONE OF THESE DRIED HERBS OR FLOWERS (BAY LEAF, CHAMOMILE, LAVENDER, LEMON VERBENA, PEPPERMINT, ROSEMARY, ROSES, SAGE, OR SCENTED GERANIUMS)
6 MUSLIN BAGS

Mix the oatmeal and herbs in a bowl.

Put the mixture into the muslin bags and tie the twine, making a bow or loop.

After you have filled the tub, swish the sachet through hot water a few times.

Hang the sachet on the tap to dry, as it can be used several times.

MAKES 6 SMALL BATH SACHETS

What was Paradise? but a Garden, an Orchard of Trees and Herbs, full of pleasure, and nothing there but delights. . . . What can your eye desire to see, your nose to smell, your mouth to take that is not to be had in an Orchard?

WILLIAM LAWSON

He who makes a garden
Works hand in hand with God.

DOUGLAS MALLOCH

A garden that one makes oneself becomes associated with one's personal history and that of one's friends, interwoven with one's tastes, preferences, and character, and constitutes a sort of unwritten, but withal manifest, autobiography. Show me your garden, provided it be your own, and I will tell you what you are like.

ALFRED AUSTIN

Earth laughs in flowers.

RALPH WALDO EMERSON

And se the fresshe floures how they sprynge

GEOFFREY CHAUCER

For art may err, but Nature cannot miss.

JOHN DRYDEN

Oh, let it go. Let the plants fight their own battle.

KATHARINE F. WHITE

Smell is the sense of the imagination.

JEAN-JACQUES ROUSSEAU

To create a little flower is the labour of ages.

WILLIAM BLAKE

Won't you come into my garden?
I would like my roses to see you.

RICHARD SHERIDAN

## Victorian Flower Balls

*Victorian flower balls,
covered in fresh flowers, can be suspended from
the ceiling over dining tables or hung in foyers as
a welcoming gesture. If they must be made in
advance, use dried flowers.*

STYROFOAM BALLS,
GRAPEFRUIT- TO
MELON-SIZE

CHICKEN WIRE

PICTURE WIRE

PRETTY RIBBONS

A VARIETY OF COLORFUL
FLOWERS WITH FIRM
STEMS, SUCH AS
CARNATIONS,
DAFFODILS, DAHLIAS,
DAISIES, MARIGOLDS,
ROSES, ZINNIAS

🌢 Wrap the ball with chicken wire.

🌢 Hook a length of wire at the top, which
will then be used to hang the ball.

🌢 Cover the wire with ribbon, making a
single or double bow at the top of the ball.

🌣 Cut the flower stems so they are all the
same length—about ¾ inch.

🌢 Making holes with a knitting needle, push
the flowers into the ball, covering it.

🌣 Spray with water and refrigerate for a short
period. Suspend before guests arrive.

No occupation is so delightful to me as the culture of the earth . . . and no culture comparable to that of the garden . . . But though an old man, I am but a young gardener.

THOMAS JEFFERSON

Some tulips last so long you could almost dust them off, and others you can't trust overnight.

CONSTANCE SPRY

Every blossoming square in cottage gardens seen from the flying windows of the train has its true and touching message for the traveller, and stirs delightful thought.

MRS. FRANCIS KING

It gives one a sudden start in going down a barren, stony street, to see upon a narrow strip of grass, just within the iron fence, the radiant dandelion, shining in the grass, like a spark dropped from the sun.

HENRY WARD BEECHER

The world is too much with us; late and soon,
Getting and spending, we lay waste our powers:
Little we see in Nature that is ours.

WILLIAM WORDSWORTH

The maple wears a gayer scarf,
    The field a scarlet gown,
Lest I should be old fashioned
    I'll put a trinket on.

EMILY DICKINSON

A house with daffodils in it is a house lit up,
whether or no the sun be shining outside.
Daffodils in a green bowl—and let it snow
if it will.

A. A. MILNE

Ever since I could remember anything, flowers have been like dear friends to me, comforters, inspirers, powers to uplift and to cheer.

CELIA THAXTER

# Herbal Pick-Me-Ups

To me luxury is little things —like reading the latest issue of my favorite magazine while my feet are soaking in an herbal foot bath, or rubbing scented oil on arms and legs after a particularly strenuous day.

## LEMON FOOT BATH

🌿 Boil 8 cups of water. Add 5 sprigs of fresh or 10 sprigs of dried lemon verbena leaves (rosemary can also be used).

🌿 Let stand till water is warm and comfortable.

🌿 Pour into a bowl and soak your feet from 10 to 20 minutes. Rinse off with cold water.

## ROSEMARY RUB

🌿 To 2 cups of odorless rubbing alcohol, add ½ cup of freshly crushed rosemary leaves. You can also use lemon verbena leaves or lavender.

🌿 Put in a covered jar and let sit for a week.

🌿 Strain out the herbs and put in a bottle.

🌿 Rub gently on arms and legs.

*The Amen! of Nature is
always a flower.*

OLIVER WENDELL HOLMES